MY LOVE IS A POEM WRITTEN FOR YOU

Written by

Joseph Stanners

My Inspiration

I wrote a poem a day

All about you in every which way

I wrote what is on my mind

To leave all my worries behind

Whether it be a poem about love

Or a sexy eye-popping wow

Your always on my mind

And showing me how

So, let me say thank you

To the one who inspires

It to be true

Your smile

Your smile is what got me

So shy and so cute

Your eyes are what pulled me

So far and so deep

Your lips are what felt me

So soft and so sweat

Your words are what kept me

So warm and so neat

Your love is what made me

So full and so complete

Dance

Let us dance our first dance

So, we can begin our forever romance

We will kiss all day and night

And never lose each others sight

With my arms wrapped around you

My heart in the lead

Ill twirl you around

For your love is all I need

Thinking of you

When I think of you, I often get

Swept away into a new world

And new dimension

A place that has no rules or time

Just us forever eyes locked

With smiles big and wide

Lost in each other

I can stay there forever

Wild

You were born under the stars

Always wanting to live free

You were wild and content

Then one day you met me

You fell in love with the romance

But I was only being me

You did not know this existed

The feelings that came to be

You said I saved you from the wild

But it was you that really rescued me

Can't

I can't fall out of

What's the word?

The feeling that

Can't describe

I see your face

And can't hide

The love

I hold inside

Love song

Our love is a song

Our hearts sing it so

When we are together

It always shows

From our wide shining smiles

And sweet little kisses

We move to our music

Arms wrapped in each other

Always adding new lines

Making our love song

Now and forever

A smile you made

You're the smile that won't go away

What have you done?

It happens so quickly

It takes no effort

And is always fun

This smile breaks out

With just one thought

As you're always on my mind

A smile looks good on me

I must let you know

This is what you have done

Let me love you

Let me love you

Only you

All of you

The way I can

The way you want

To make you mine

Till the end of time

Let me love you

The magic

The magic is us

Carefree with no clothes on

Hands all over each others body's

Passionately kissing with intent

Together in the moment

Holding nothing back

Making love all night

Forever empowering

The magic in us

Lost in love

I want to get lost in our love
Swept away to our special place
With our hearts beating together
Slowing down this crazy life's pace
I want to get lost in our love
That feeling of forever bliss
Looking into your eyes
Knowing we are made for each other
And seal it with a kiss

The music

The music we make

In the bedroom

Will wake any

Sleeping neighbours

We play our favourite song

Full of pleasure

And delight

Always making love

To each other

Every night

Your lips

I fell in love with your lips

The way they kiss mine

How they widen when they see me

Moisten when I come near

The way they feel on my skin

And over my body

How they kiss me on the way down

They are an addiction

That I'm glad I found

Your lips are true beauty

Bringing out an inspiration

Whenever they kiss mine

Lock it in

I worked so hard to find you

I'm never letting you go

You are the beat of my soul

I will let everyone know

My body is yours sealed with a kiss

My mind is forever on you

Never to let a second miss

Take my heart and lock it in

Throw away the key

And let this love begin

Today

Today I will kiss you

Full of passion

And intent

Kisses that will take

Your breath away

And bring your mind

To a melt

It will sweep you away

To that special place

With just a kiss, that

I will give you today

Speak to me

When you speak to me
My soul is there to listen
You say all the right words
That it had been missing
Its like you knew all along
How to reach it
Knowing exactly how I feel
Our souls are connected
Your voice has revealed
A passion inside me
That only true soulmates
Can yield

To my love

To my love

I often write about you

The way you look

The way you feel

The way you sound

Makes the words real

When I see you

I will let you know

My words will tell it so

But while I wait

I will write you a poem

And not let these feelings

Have me alone

Blue eyes

Your blue eyes are my weakness
My heart let's me know
I can look at them forever
The calm in my breath tells me so
Please don't ever look away
I don't know what I would do
For your blue eyes are my weakness
And a part that keeps me whole

Breath of fresh air

You are a breath of fresh air

Giving my mind the needed ease

I was searching in the fog

Only to be broken and brought to my knees

As I looked up into the stars

Begging to be set free

The fog started to lift

As you stood there in front of me

Breathing life into my body

Opening a new path to succeed

We both made it out together

Your breath was all I would need

Waiting

I've been waiting to fall in love

Not knowing how to get there

It always seemed to skip me

And gave it to someone else

Then one day we crossed paths

Never had I seen such a perfect match

My time has finally come

As I knew this love

Had me waiting

So, it can forever last

Falling for you

I fall for you deeper everyday
Your beautiful eyes make it so
Your smile wonderfully captivating
I can help but look shy
I fall for you deeper everyday
Your body beautifully mesmerizing
Your movements take control
I fall for you deeper everyday
Your voice calming and sweet
I await on your every word
To make my heart feel complete
I fall for you deeper everyday
Your soul always touching mine
It was the energy that brought us together
As you are amazing and one of a kind

One more minute

I just need one more minute

To hold you and kiss you

Just one more minute

To tell you I love you

Just one more minute

To get lost in that feeling

Just one more minute

To be at ease

Just one more minute

Right now, and forever

Morning sunshine

You are so beautiful
In the morning
With the sun shining
On your smiling face
Thoughts of last nights
Kisses on your mind
And a tingling feeling
I left behind

Love poem

I thought about texting you a poem

But I wrote a one instead

I will wait for the right time

To let you read it

As this will make you feel

Love in the head

Its full of wonderful feelings

Smiling thoughts

Emotion overflowing

And a love inspiring warmth

Soulmate

Today I found my soulmate
My heartbeat right around you
The feelings can't be explained
But they find a way to reach you
As I move at a different pace
Smile when I look upon your face
In the aura around you, I am lost
My soul has fallen in love
Because today I found you
And tomorrow is the first day
I will never be alone

Love me back

I love the way you love me back

Your love has captured my soul

You touch me ever so right

Giving me feelings, I can't control

When you make love to me

My mind begins to fade

I can't stand straight

As me knees have given away

The way you love

The way you care

I will always hold it close

It's the way you love me back

That keeps my heart beating the most

Love you back

Let me love you back

And see it in your eyes

Giving you the feelings

You can not hide

Let me touch your heart

When I hold you

Cleans your soul

When I kiss you

And see that

Everlasting glow

Moments

Take my heart and guide it there

To the place we both have no underwear

Fool around and tickle my feet

Kiss my lips and tell me they're sweet

Look me in the eyes calling them pretty

Talk all night and say something witty

Make me laugh until I cry

Hold me in your arms never to say goodbye

These are the moments I live by

In this beautiful life of mine

Eyes Closed

You look beautiful with your eyes closed

Smiling just a slight

Laying there teasing

I think I may have to bite

My hands will rush over your body

As your lungs gasp for air

The pleasure will overwhelm you

When you surrender to my hands care

As I sense your enjoyment

Your body has you begging for more

So, close your eyes and dare me

And I will promise

To please you all night

Desire

I feel you looking at me

I see the fire inside

You want to be my desire

And know the pleasures that I hide

So, let me touch your body

Take over your mind

When we go all in

It will fuel that fire inside

Letting it burn so hot

You will never be the same

Making you my desire

And I your never-ending flame

Crazy for you

I am crazy for you

This you have let out

You're always showering me with kisses

And smiles that shout

You give me this wonderful feeling

That I can't live without

You are in control of my body

With your sense of seduction

Always leaving my mind in wonder

From your one-of-a-kind impression

The way you handle me with care

Just being your natural way

Makes me crazy for you

Each day

Fallen for you

I've seen what love looks like

I felt it in my heart

Looking deep into your eyes

I knew I never wanted to be apart

With a sense of belonging

We hold each other tight

Make passionate love

And kiss throughout the night

With whispers in our ears

We speak the words we both adore

I have fallen for you

Don't ever loose my sight

Love spell

The spell was cast

The mood was set

Together locked in pleasure

Our minds faded then met

We gave into the feeling

Never to let a second go

Body's left with tingles

Smiles on our faces to show

Wake up kiss

Can we wake up and kiss?

These are the moments

I always miss

Whenever we're together

Life always feels like this

Totally content

To lay there

For hours

All from a kiss

When we wake up

Together

In bed

Smile I found

I found a smile

Shining bright it grew

When our souls touch

This shows me its true

I will forever be blessed

With a beautiful smile

Because what I found

Was you

Meet you there

I will always meet you there
In the place we call our own
All the time I have spent with you
Shows how far our love has grown
This love has changed us
Brought us to this special place
I will always meet you there
And be lost in our soul's embrace

In a mess

I love your hair

In a mess

With my hands

Running through

Pulling and twisting

To my delight

Knowing I made it that way

Puts a smile on my face

And I know

That you secretly

Like it too

Flame

You lit my flame

From the moment we met

Eyes locked together

Every second we get

Minds lost in wonder

Our souls have let

Together in love

Flaming hearts will set

Whispers

Our body's have

Become one

Letting our emotions

Fully run free

The whispers in the night

I love you

Are now

The only thing

Hy heart can't live

Without

Snuggles

Let us get some snuggles

Dive right into bed

Pile up the pillows

And rest your heads

Hold each other close

Breath in the air around us

Fall asleep with hearts

Beating together

Seeing you in my dreams

Tonight, and forever

Grab me

Grab me on the way by

Twirl me how I like

Have your eyes locked on me

With teeth ready to bite

You know what I want

So, treat me right

And whisper in my ear

Let's make love tonight

Laugh

Laugh all day

Have fun all night

Kiss me and hold me right

Show me all your beauty

As you set it free

And feel my heart

Pounding for you

Laughing along side too

Must

Our hearts did not lie

The first time we met

I love spending time with you

Every chance I get

Its more then addiction

Deeper than lust

I fell in love with you

And now having you in my life

Is a must

Dance all night

Grab my hips and pull me in
Let's start this night off dancing
Seduce me with your beautiful eyes
Temp me with those luscious lips
Touch my body with your magic hands
Whisk me away to that special place
Holding each other in that moment
Making love to the music
And dance together all night

Inner flame

With the flow

Of pleasure

Running through

My veins

You make my heart

Beat wild

From lighting

My inner flame

You are beautiful

You are beautiful
These words will always be told
My body is filled with warmth
When ever I have yours to hold
Looking deep into your eyes
This always comes to mind
You are beautiful
And together we will live this life
With our souls intertwined

Walk with me

Walk with me

In this life of mine

Hand in hand

We will make our way

Let me tell you

How much I love you

And let everybody see

That when you walk with me

I am so proud to have you

The smile on my face

Will say it all

Be mine

You are beautiful and sweet

You make my life complete

My heart is bursting with love

This smile on my face

Is what you create

When I look upon your

Gorgeous eyes

Let me sweep you off your feet

Take you in my arms

Kiss you, laugh with you

Tell you how much I love you

Then ask for you to be mine

With me

Laugh with me

Smile with me

Take me to the other side

Pleasure me

Tease me

Touch your skin to mine

Excite my body

Open my mind

Tell me you love me

While taking my hand

To be yours

In this life so grand

I am yours

Tonight, I am yours

To let your sexual desires free

So, undress me slowly

Reveal my treasures

And release the pleasure

Locked inside of me

Run your hands over my curves

Pull my hair and tell me I am yours

Take me with passion

In the heat of the night

When we climax together

Ill whisper these words

I am yours

Your eyes

I love the way

Your eyes look at mine

They speak in ways of wonder

My soul is blessed

My spirt is cleansed

With one look I get from them

They show me love

They show me laughter

I see a future

And a happily ever after

Meant to see

As I lay beside you

With a smile on my face

I have visions of happiness

And a feeling of grace

I see a love that is real

With two souls becoming one

These are brilliant moments

That show the truth

Love does not blind

It reveals the way

We are meant to see

Come to bed

Come to bed with me

Lay your head next to mine

Touch my body

And warm it over time

Fall asleep in my arms

Not to wake up from any alarms

As these nights we spend together

Are amazing and always the best

Because when you come to bed with me

I know I found my eternal rest

My love is a poem

My love is a poem

Written for you

I have memorized every line

The thoughts and feelings

Are always on my mind

This poem gives me inspiration

Even on the darkest days

For my love is a poem

That I write line by line

Flowing happily from my heart

As this love is you

The soulmate that

Inspires a poem

That has come true

Undress

You watch me undress
Waiting for what's to come
You say I am beautiful
But you are the one
That captured my heart
Giving it the love, it needs
While allowing me to be
The one you adore
Getting undressed
For your eyes only
Too see

Falling for you

I want to fall in

The deepest way

Explore the depths

That make you

I want to feel you

All of you

Touch every part

Of your body

I want to make love

To you passionately

Take you to places

You have never known

I want this and

Will make it my own

Warm your body

I will warm your body

Just come close

Touch your skin to mine

As it craves you the most

When your warm we will kiss

Your lips I forever miss

I will hold you tight hold you right

And never let you out of my sight

Wall of beauty

There was a wall of beauty

Surrounding you and I

We twirled and danced in it that day

Never did time feel so still

If only I could stop it there

And feel the energy around us

While I look at your smiling face

And embrace the beauty

Of the wall we made

I would forever be in grace

Trees in the wind

The trees blow in the wind

On a warm summer night

Having just made love

The stars shine bright

We sit outside naked

Watching the trees blow in the wind

With smiles on our faces

A calming peace in our heart

Tonight, we discover

How madly in love we are

With each other

Lay me down

Lay me down tonight

Seduce my mind

And take over my body

Show me how those hands

Can caress my heart

Make love to it

Like it's a work of art

Lay me down tonight

Showering my body

With delicate kisses

Hitting all the right spots

That you know it misses

Lay me down tonight

And every night

So, I can hear the words

I love you

Before my eyes shut

What love looks like

We are what love looks like

As we dance in the rain

Twirling and laughing

With only smiles to gain

We are the picture of warmth

On a cold snowing night

Wrapped up in each other

Until first sunlight

We are what love looks like

We feel it in our hearts

What we do together

Will set us apart

Showing our love

To be inspiring

For all to see

Through the fields

You are beautiful today
Just the way you are
Walking through the fields
Shining like a star
Nature is where you belong
Its your healing space
Watching you walk
Through the fields
Puts a smile on my face

Dreams

Tonight, I will dream

And tomorrow it will come true

Anything is possible

When I dream with you

From the first morning light

To the darkness of night

Dreams will come true

Living in the moment

Whenever I am

With you

Crave

I crave for the taste of your lips

The touch of your skin

Your breath on my neck

The rush of air I breathe in

Kisses all over my body

Eyes wide with excitement

Smiles from ear to ear

And giggles of laughter

Ending in pleasure

I crave to make love

To you forever

Love you tonight

I love you; I love you
I love you tonight
Looking up into the sky
I know I won the fight
You fell from the stars
With love at first sight
Making our hearts grow stronger
Leading us to new heights
I love you; I love you
I love you tonight

Connected

You calm my soul

When you look at me

Take my breath

When our eyes connect

You make my heartbeat faster

With that pretty smile

You keep my body warm

Holding on to yours

For a while

You and I are connected

Our souls are together

In this life

Now and forever

Moments

When I am with you
A minute feels like a second
An hour feels like a minute
Time passes by quickly
But I only need a moment
From time to time
To tell you all the ways I love you
And how I want you to be mine

Two Halves

You are the half

That makes me whole

The one I have been searching for

You touched my soul

The moment we met

To repay your love

I will forever be

In your dept

Today and always

Our two halves

Will be set

Embrace

You drive me wild

To say I like you is a bit mild

You're not shy or afraid

You know how to get your way

When you show me your seduction

And have me under control

I am lost in the moment

Embracing your soul

Feeling the love

That we share together

You are my

You are my body

You are my soul

You are my everything

That I behold

You are my light

You are my guide

You are the love

That I never hide

You are my friend

You are my love

You are every word

Spoken above

Morning kisses

We wake up to morning kisses

And soft hand caressing

With eyes barely awake

Whispers on our breath

That please the mind

Has our hips stirring and

Starting to grind

The first kisses of the day

Leave a lasting impression

Till our lips meet again

And kiss at first sight

It's the early morning kisses

That set the tone

For our love

To take flight

Set your wild free

I do not wish to tame you
Only set your wild free
You are uniquely beautiful
And bring out that wild in me
The way you see life
Is an inspiration I'm lucky to see
You have this fire in your soul
With a passion that exudes
My heart and warm words can only
Wish you to be successful
And let that wild in you
Continue to flow

The smell of your skin

The smell of your skin

The air I breath in

Tingles the senses

As a wonderful feeling begins

Rushes of excitement

Pules in the veins

Taking a deep breath

I'm lost for days

The sweet smell of your skin

Was the start of it all

My heart had no chance

With one inhale, I did fall

Pleasure inside

The pleasure inside me
Is only for you
I hold on to it
For the times to show you its true
With a rush of excitement
On any given night
The pleasure inside me
Will bathe your soul in light
And calm your mind
While our hearts
Become intertwined

Object of affection

I have been an object of affection
That only a few have had a taste
I stand here smiling
As I look at your face
You see me in a different way
Let me be a little crazy
And hold on to the moments
That's only you and I
This beautiful life that we created
Was not just a lucky chance
But a loving creation
Of two spirits aligned
And a love that is
Truly divine

Flow

With the flow

Of pleasure

Running through

My veins

You make my heart

Beat wild

From lighting

My inner flame

The feeling it left

It has been an addiction

From the first exhaled breath

Breathing in the air around you

I absorbed your aura

And now I crave for the feeling it left

To be in that place together

With our body's losing all control

We fall in love with each other

Knowing that this life

Is ours to behold

Loves eternal chase

I want a love

That drives me wild

Having my heart burst

From my chest

I want that instant smile

When I see your face

A tear from my eye

When I think of

Your beautiful grace

I want a love

That drives me wild

Sweeps me of my feet

To that special place

We call our own

Living free

Lost in loves eternal chase

If you were a word

If you were a word
I know it would be love
Ever since I met you
Its all my mind knows how to say
When ever you are near
This love carries me away
Leaving a lasting impression
Today and every day
If you were a word
The word would be love

Hair and eyes

I can't get over

How I already knew

From the first moment

I laid eyes on you

I was in trouble

As you are the one

Who is gorgeous and fun

Catching my attention

Being amazed in wonder

All this from

The first gander

Of your beautiful hair

And eyes

Sugar skin

Not knowing where my teeth

And my mind even begins

I find myself loosing control

Nibbling on your sweet sugar skin

From the first touch of my lips

I feel the desire to bite in

Watching your body shake

Only heightens the addiction

And always has me

Going back for more

Leaving my mark

As I fill my mouth

With the taste of your

Sweet sugar skin

Dreams

Tonight, I will dream

And tomorrow it will come true

Anything is possible

When I am with you

From the first morning light

To the darkness of night

Dreams will come true

Living in the moment

Whenever I am

With you

Wings of love

When love gives you wings
You take them and fly
Don't be afraid
The love never dies
It flows in your direction
And I along for the ride
Soaring intently
Always reaching for the sky
Knowing no limits
Is the reason why
When love gives you wings
Your heart will thank you
With smiles so wide

Best line

Give me your best line

To catch my attention

Tell me I'm fine

To feed the obsession

Make me crave your wicked mind

And tell me how you

Would take me

Leaving no detail behind

I want to feel what its like

To be yours

Letting you control my body

Stimulating my mind

With your best line

To get me in bed

Subtle looks

A subtle look

A knowing smile

I find myself

Gazing over you a while

A familiar place

That I call home

When I look at you

I no longer feel alone

You are my friend

And my lover

I can not think

Of a better place

To spend my forever

Love Story

Let's write our love story

Making it the greatest ever told

Now that we are in this life

We can let it unfold

Unraveling the mystery's

From a passion so bold

Writing our history

And showing the world

What love looks like

In the greatest love story

Ever told

My love

I will always love you

I will always hold you close

I will always cherish your body

As I love you the most

You showed me true love

You showed me that its real

You showed me that's its alright

To tell you how I feel

I will love you tomorrow

I will love you today

I will love you in the moment

These words I will always say

You are my beautiful

You are my light

You are my love

And the one I will spend my life

Love comes easy

It's a special feeling

When you meet the one

The one who sees you

Takes your breath away

Beats your heart a little faster

Has you believing in that

Happily, ever after

Because I know its true

Love just comes easy

Ever since I met you

One day

Then one day

The most beautiful girl came into my life

And I said I would go the extra mile

Just to see you for a little while

And be lost in your embrace

Taken back by your beauty

When your soft lips kiss my face

To be in your presence

My heart would be yours to take

As this is the love

I've been waiting for

The day has finally arrived

And all you had to do

Was to say hi

Give me a life (a new chapter)

Give me a life

That's worthy of me

One full of love

And plenty of laughter

Setting me free of

This disaster

Of not living another day

Without you

As today I will ask you

To be my forever

Giving me a life

That I sought after

Letting my heart be yours

Closing this lonely chapter

Manufactured by Amazon.ca
Bolton, ON